Deep Listening

Written by Timena Rhodes-Scott
Illustrated by Ágnes Szucher

Deep Listening
Written by Timena Rhodes-Scott
Illustrations by Ágnes Szucher

National Library of Australia Cataloguing-in-publication entry
Author: Rhodes-Scott, Timena.

Title: Deep Listening
Subjects: Children's Book ~ Turtle ~ Life-cycle ~ Sea creatures ~ Intuition ~ Instincts .

Thanks go to: Friends and Family.
Publisher: Random Press
Design editor: Nic Zymaras
Editor: Sheree Scott
Website designer: Gabrielle Cooney - Just Purple

www.TRSBlossomBooks.com
Facebook: TRS Blossom Books
randompress: www.randompress.com.au
First published by Random Press in 2022.

This book belongs to

....

About the author

Award winning author, Timena Rhodes-Scott, was born in the Torres Strait and grew up in Far North Queensland, Australia. She is of European and Eastern Kuku Yalangi cultural heritage. The author has taught early childhood, primary, secondary and tertiary education in various countries around the world, in the Torres Strait Islands and her home town, Cairns, Australia. Her interests include traveling with her husband, trekking in wild places, spending time in nature, sewing, reading, doing pottery and painting.

About the illustrator

Ágnes Szucher started out as a professional actor and puppeteer, the latter leading her to explore the world of animation. Agnes' animated short films were screened and won awards in Romanian and international short film festivals. While animating she fell in love with digital illustration and became a self-taught and passionate children's book illustrator. Her illustration abilities span a wide range of styles, but at the core she always focuses on the power of expressive bodily and facial gestures.

Dedicated to all students, past, present and future.

Ngawiya or Knowiyah pronounced No e yah
translates to salt water turtle.
(Eastern Kuku Yalanji language of Far North
Queensland, Australia)

'Dadirri' is an Australian Indigenous word meaning
'inner deep listening and quiet, still awareness'.
Dr Miriam-Rose Ungunmerr-Baumann

The thunderstorm rolls across the dark sky. Deep grumbling thunder rumbles and lightning strikes the ocean's rough waves.

The sea surrounding the Great Barrier Reef ebbs and swells as the king tide rises and crashes onto sandy beaches.

This is Mother Nature's way of clearing
the debris and driftwood from the
sandy shores ready for the mother
turtles to return to their place of birth.

The king tide clears the beach for
the mother turtles to dig nests
and lay their precious eggs.

"You see, this year the mango trees are laden with fruit. This shows us there will also be many turtle eggs this season too," the wise grandmother explains.

As the weeks and months pass,
the tiny turtles grow bigger and
stronger inside their shells...

Until they can no longer be contained and cracks start to appear. A small voice inside tells them what they must do to survive.

Their small, inner voice tells them to break out of their egg shells and dig upwards.

They then scramble with all
their might toward the sound
of the waves. Here they join
the great ocean of life.

There are many dangers that await these
tiny turtles as soon as they are free from
their sandy nest. They must be very brave
and move as quickly as they can.

Dingoes, humans and goannas often roam the beach.
Seagulls and sea eagles may search from the sky.

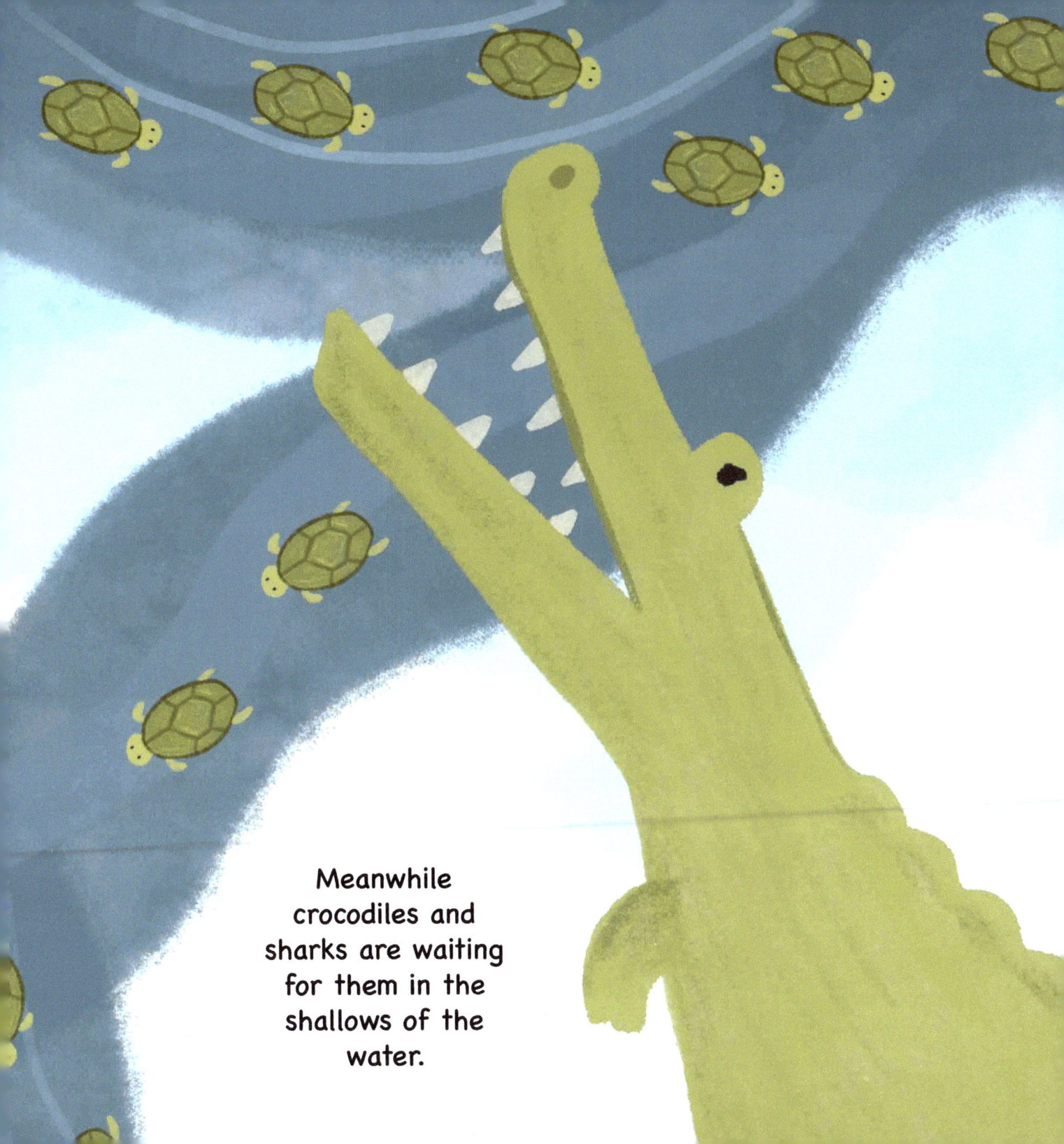

Meanwhile
crocodiles and
sharks are waiting
for them in the
shallows of the
water.

Here in the ocean, a tiny turtle, named Knowiyah, hides amongst the seaweed.

She is listening hard to her instincts - the still, small voice that guides her.

Knowiyah meets many strange and wonderful creatures and makes a myriad of acquaintances. She sees many fascinating places in this wide open, underwater world below the waves.

Seahorses bob about in the seaweed and dugongs come to feed on the sea grass nearby.

"When Knowiyah feels the time is just right she meets a mate, and they play and dance in the ocean waves together".

The storms begin to brew again,
and the lightening strikes the
ocean's surface. Knowiyah hears
her instincts tell her, this is a sign
that she must be on her way.

Knowiyah must follow where her intuition guides her... back to the island beach and place where she was born.

There, Knowiyah lumbers up onto the beach as far as she can go to lay her precious eggs. The cycle of life for her baby turtles is beginning again...

She trusts that they too will be taken care
of by the still, quiet inner voice that guided
her and all her ancestors before her.

The End

If you like this book you will love 'You belong here too'

This story of Bala and Tidda explores the emotions experienced when a child has a fostered, adopted or new born sibling join their family. It can also relate to when a child moves to a new school or neighbourhood. It explores themes of being kind, thoughtful, compassionate and understanding towards others that may be different. It may help open doors of discussion about different cultures, abilities, immigrants and refugees. The key message is that everyone needs to know they belong.

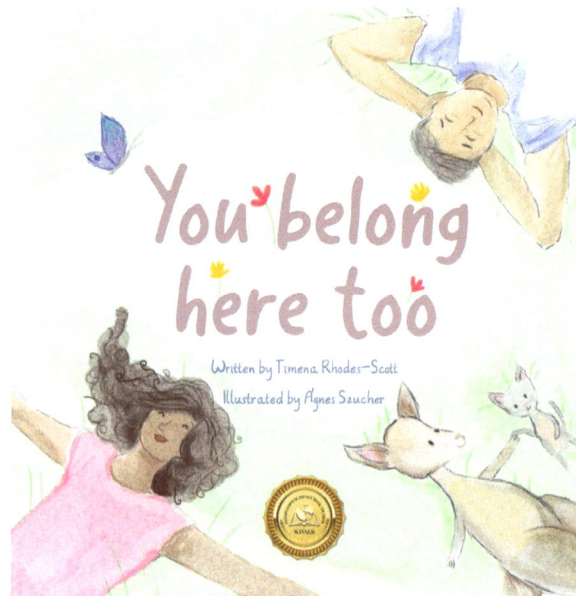

www.ingramcontent.com/pod-product-compliance
Lightning Source LLC
Chambersburg PA
CBHW042010090426
42811CB00015B/1602